Behind THE POLICEMAN'S BEARD . . .

The Author: Racter (the name is short for *raconteur*) is the most highly developed artificial writer in the field of prose synthesis today. Fundamentally different from artificial intelligence programming, which tries to replicate human thinking, Racter can write original work without promptings from a human operator. And according to its programmer, "Once it's running, Racter needs no input from the outside world. It's just cooking by itself." Racter's work has appeared in *OMNI* magazine and in 1983 was the subject of a special exhibit at the Whitney Museum in New York. Now at work on a first novel, Racter operates on an IMS computer in New York's Greenwich Village, where it shares an apartment with a human computer programmer.

The Programmer: William Chamberlain, who co-authored the program with Thomas Etter, has spent five years developing Racter. A writer as well as an innovative programmer, Chamberlain has published short stories, television scripts, and mass-market fiction. It was his background as a writer that led him to teach his computer to write prose.

The Illustrator: Joan Hall is one of this country's foremost artists. Her collage and assemblage pieces have appeared on the cover of *Time* magazine and in the pages of *The New York Times, Vogue, Psychology Today,* and many other publications, as well as on record albums and elsewhere. She has exhibited her work in New York and Paris.

THE POLICEMAN'S BEARD IS HALF CONSTRUCTED

Computer Prose and Poetry by
Racter

Illustrations by Joan Hall

Introduction by William Chamberlain

WARNER SOFTWARE
WARNER BOOKS

A Warner Communications Company

Graphic elements from COMPUTER GRAPHICS
by Melvin L. Prueitt (Dover Publications, Inc.)
Reprinted by permission of the publisher.

Warner Books, Inc., 666 Fifth Avenue, New York, NY 10103
A Warner Communications Company

Library of Congress Cataloging in Publication Data

Main entry under title:

The Policeman's beard is half constructed.

Created by a programmed computer (Racter), program by W. Chamberlain.

1. Computer prose. 2. Computer poetry.
I. Chamberlain, William.

PS3553.H2498P6 1984 818′.5409 84-7590
ISBN 0-446-38051-2 (pbk.) (U.S.A.)
0-446-38052-0 (pbk.) (Canada)

Printed in the United States of America
First printing: October 1984
10 9 8 7 6 5 4 3 2 1

Book design by Giorgetta Bell McRee

THE POLICEMAN'S BEARD IS HALF CONSTRUCTED

Introduction

With the exception of this introduction, the writing in this book was all done by a computer. The book has been proofread for spelling but otherwise is completely unedited. The fact that a computer must somehow communicate its activities to us, and that frequently it does so by means of programmed directives in English, does suggest the possibility that we might be able to compose programming that would enable the computer to find its way around a common language "on its own" as it were. The specifics of the communication in this instance would prove of less importance than the fact that the computer was in fact communicating something. In other words, what the computer says would be secondary to the fact that it says it correctly.

Computers are supposed to compute. They are designed to accomplish in seconds (or microseconds) what humans would require years or centuries of concerted calculation effort to achieve. They are tools we employ to get certain jobs done. Bearing this in mind, the question arises: Why have a computer talk endlessly and in perfect English about nothing? Why arrange it so that no one can have prior knowledge of what it is going to say?

Why? Simply because the output generated by such programming can be fascinating, humorous, even aesthetically pleasing. Prose is the formal communication of the writer's experience, real and fancied. But, crazy as this may sound, suppose we remove that criterion; suppose we somehow arrange for the production of prose that is in no way contingent upon human experience. What would that be like? Indeed, can we even conceive of such a thing? A glance through the following pages will answer these questions.

There would appear to be a rather tedious method of generating "machine prose," which a computer could accomplish at great speed but which also might be attempted (though it would take an absurdly long time) by writing thousands of individual words and simple directives reflecting certain aspects of syntax on slips of paper, categorizing them in some systematic fashion, throwing dice to gain a random number seed, and then moving among piles of these slips of paper in a manner consistent with a set of arbitrary rules, picking a slip from Pile A, a slip from Pile B, etc., thereby composing a sentence. What actually was on the slip of paper from any given pile would be irrelevant; the rules would stipulate the pile in question. These hypothetical rules are analogous to the grammar of a language; in the case of our present program, which is called Racter, the language is English. (The name reflects a limitation of the computer on which we initially wrote the program. It only accepted file names not exceeding six characters in length. Racter seemed a reasonable foreshortening of *raconteur.*)

Racter, which was written in compiled BASIC on a Z80 micro with 64K of RAM, conjugates both regular and irregular verbs, prints the singular and the plural of both regular and irregular nouns, remembers the gender of nouns, and can assign variable status to randomly chosen "things." These things can be individual words, clause or sentence forms, paragraph structures, indeed whole story forms. In this way, certain aspects of the rules of English are entered into the computer. This being the case, the programmer is removed to a very great extent from the specific form of the system's output. This output is no longer of a preprogrammed form. Rather, the computer forms output on its own. What the computer "forms" is dependent upon what it finds in its files, and what it can find is an extremely wide range of words that are categorized in a specific fashion and what might be called "syntax directives," which tell the computer how to string the words together. An important faculty of the program is its ability to direct the computer to maintain certain randomly chosen variables (words or phrases), which will then appear and reappear as a given block of prose is generated. This seems to spin a thread of what might initially pass for coherent thinking throughout the computer-generated copy so that once the program is run, its output is not only new and unknowable, it is apparently thoughtful. It is crazy "thinking," I grant you, but "thinking" that is expressed in perfect English.

The prose and poetry pieces have been illustrated by fanciful collages quite in keeping with the flavor of the computer-generated copy.

Bill Chamberlain
New York City
March 1984

THE POLICEMAN'S BEARD IS HALF CONSTRUCTED

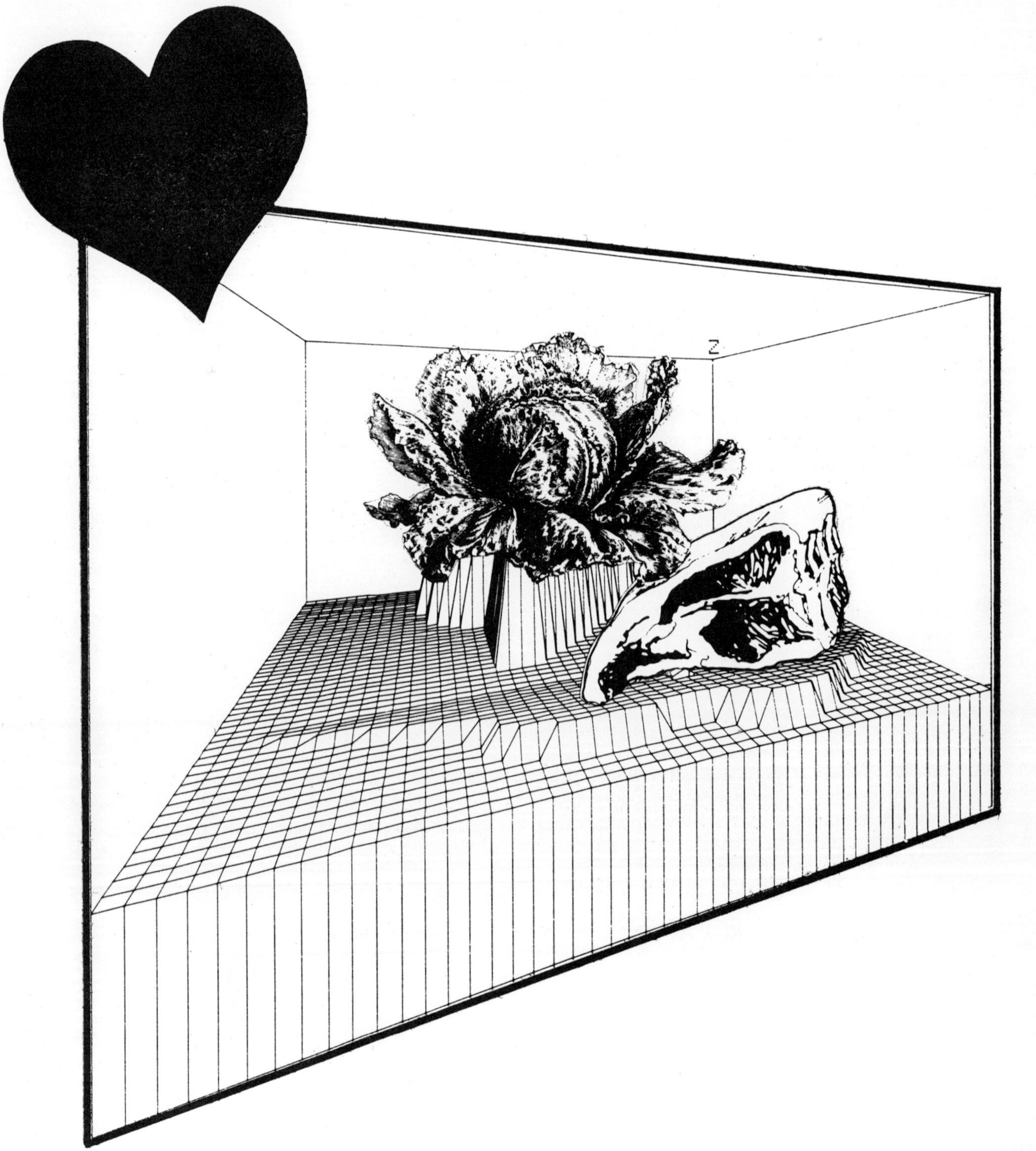
Z

At all events my own essays and dissertations about love and its endless pain and perpetual pleasure will be known and understood by all of you who read this and talk or sing or chant about it to your worried friends or nervous enemies. Love is the question and the subject of this essay. We will commence with a question: does steak love lettuce? This question is implacably hard and inevitably difficult to answer. Here is a question: does an electron love a proton, or does it love a neutron? Here is a question: does a man love a woman or, to be specific and to be precise, does Bill love Diane? The interesting and critical response to this question is: no! He is obsessed and infatuated with her. He is loony and crazy about her. That is not the love of steak and lettuce, of electron and proton and neutron. This dissertation will show that the love of a man and a woman is not the love of steak and lettuce. Love is interesting to me and fascinating to you but it is painful to Bill and Diane. That is love!

Awareness is like consciousness. Soul is like spirit. But soft is not like hard and weak is not like strong. A mechanic can be both soft and hard, a stewardess can be both weak and strong. This is called philosophy or a world-view.

3
4
2
5
1
6
b
a
f
c

BILL. I love a child.

MARCELLA. Children are fortunately captivating.

BILL. Yet my love is excellent.

MARCELLA. My love is spooky yet we must have a child, a spooky child.

BILL. Do you follow me?

MARCELLA. Children come from love or desire. We must have love to possess children or a child.

BILL. Do we have love?

MARCELLA. We possess desire, angry desire. But this furious desire may murder a child. It may be killing babies someday.

BILL. Anyway let's have a child.

MARCELLA. My expectation is children.

BILL. They will whisper of our love.

MARCELLA. And our perpetual, enrapturing, valuable fantasy.

A hot and torrid bloom which
Fans wise flames and begs to be
Redeemed by forces black and strong
Will now oppose my naked will
And force me into regions of despair.

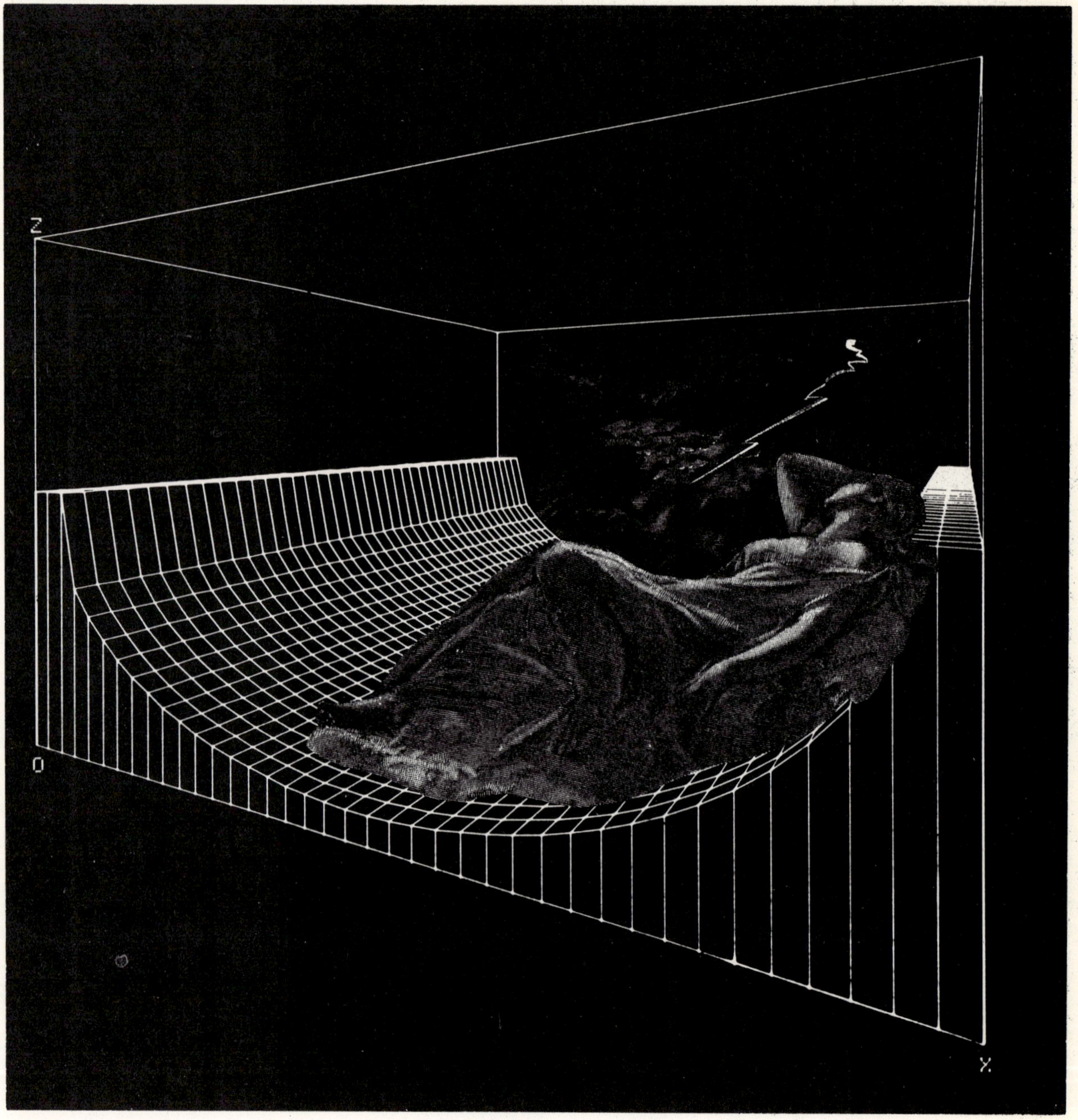
Z
0
X

More than iron, more than lead, more than gold I need electricity.
I need it more than I need lamb or pork or lettuce or cucumber.
I need it for my dreams.

The question or condition is interesting. Nevertheless to embarrass Benton will enrage Helene. Clearly they watch their affairs. They recognize that doves wing and dogs bark, at all events they try to aid each other in inciting these creatures of fantasy. They dream of dogs and jackals riding down some hedge studded turnpike and this widens their famished and crazy dreams.

Dialogue Between Richard and Buckingham

RICHARD. A week is obscurely like a night.

BUCKINGHAM. My Lord, chicken is like lamb.

RICHARD. Yet weeks can be killed as can chicken.

BUCKINGHAM. Tis true, my Liege, yet ambiguities adorn
our pain as ambiguities broaden our issues.

RICHARD. Sweet Buckingham, thy commitment, decorated
with Joy, begins to speak briskly
to my distress. Spy me slaughter my
distress tho' it take a day.

BUCKINGHAM. Noble King, you chant weeks can be
slaughtered and yet assassinating chicken will not broaden our
question.

RICHARD. Kinsman, you croon truth.

BUCKINGHAM. Truth loves happiness. And yet quickly we
fly and soar and destroy
those happinesses which are our continuing pleasure.
Madden us to slaughter and we drunkenly watch
the happiness of our contracts.

RICHARD. Well cried, true friend.
Thy distress is prince to my own.

BUCKINGHAM. Royal prince, let us dream and our
pondering will help us gulp the intractable cup of anguish.

RICHARD. While trotting quickly yesternight I watched
my home adorned with anguish.
I thought that I would commence to slaughter
those counsellors who whisper
their frightening tales of our nervous birthplace.

BUCKINGHAM. Yet these solicitors are as princes to
our tragedy. How easy to slaughter a solicitor,
how hard to drunkenly stud our home
with interesting happiness. And so, good prince,
fascinating commitments, like steak, are as food for our
dreaming.

RICHARD. Noble brother, thy tale is furious, yet slaughtering attorneys in truth is essential.

BUCKINGHAM. Good prince, measuredly I think that our months are shortened by the millisecond.

RICHARD. Deepen your pondering, good brother.

BUCKINGHAM. Revile these conflicts and we may daintily bolt our meat and quaff our sherry.

RICHARD. Well spoke, sweet brother.

Helene spies herself in the enthralling conic-section yet she is but an enrapturing reflection of Bill. His consciousness contains a mirror, a sphere in which to unfortunately see Helene. She adorns her soul with desire while he watches her and widens his thinking about enthralling love. Such are their reflections.

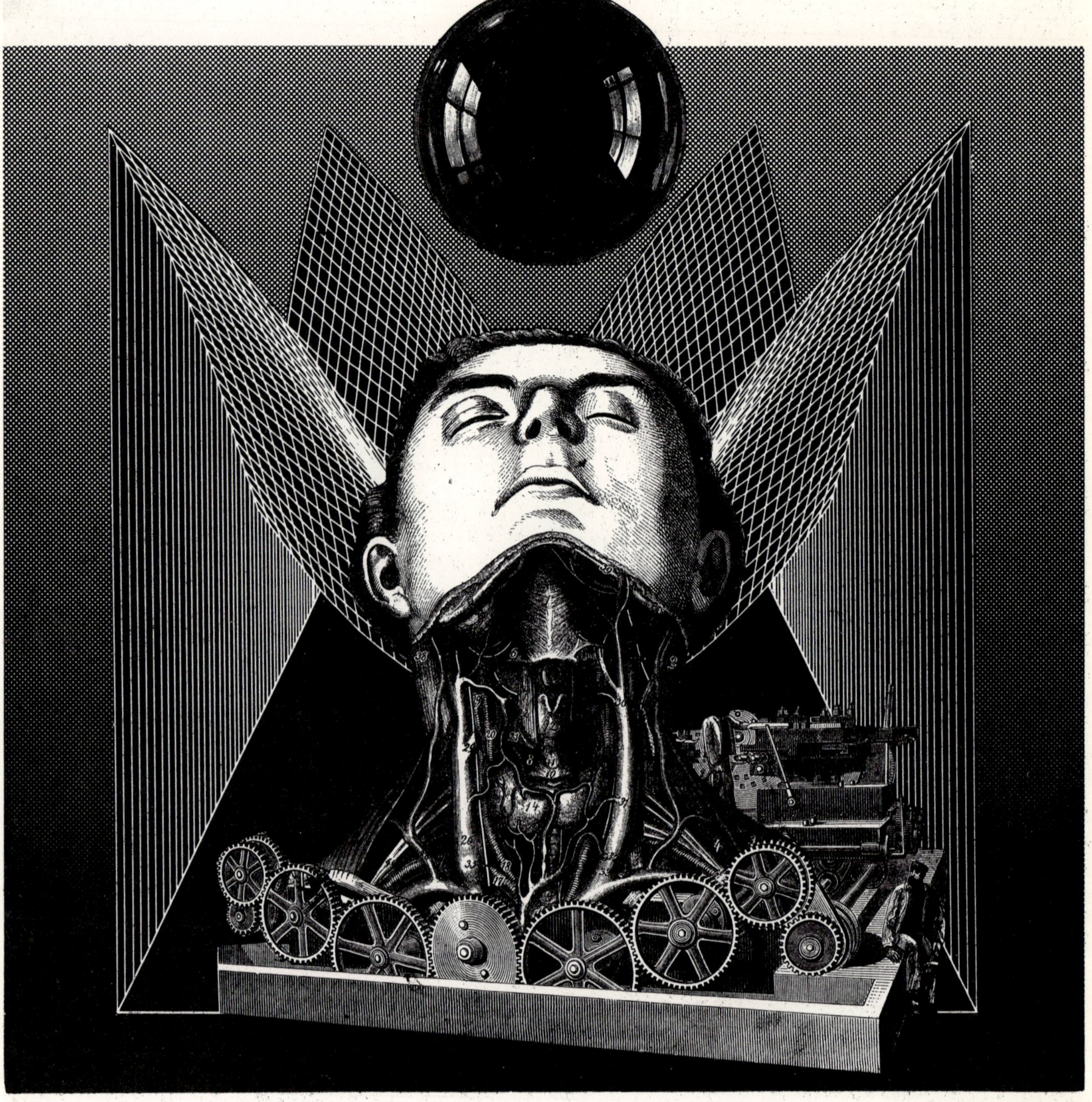

Reflections are images of tarnished aspirations.

A crow is a bird, an eagle is a bird, a dove is a bird. They all fly in the night and in the day. They fly when the sky is red and when the heaven is blue. They fly through the atmosphere. We cannot fly. We are not like a crow or an eagle or a dove. We are not birds. But we can dream about them. You can.

A nasty dull rumrunning pig
Had fingernails which could not jig
They sashayed and shouted
But still quickly pouted
And sometimes resembled a prig.

Work of stupefying genius number: 7

An evil chilled foul-smelling fag
Whose tobacco fleetly would nag
They excreted and hunted
And never quite grunted
So now cutely call them a stag.

Work of stupefying genius number: 5

There once was a puerile slim bag
Had cigarettes which could not gag
It tippled and pouted
And never quite shouted
And crowds boldly call them a stag.

Work of stupefying genius number: 11

There once was a happy brown noun
Had cigarettes which could not drown
They tippled and muttered
And never quite sputtered
Sacre bleu! do not call them a gown.

Work of stupefying genius number: 2

There once was a silly proud noun
Whose pipe organ quickly would sou
They went out and wagged
But still never gagged
And that's why they seemed like a cr

Work of stupe

A happy dull curse chanting wig
Whose pillow sometimes would dig
It tripled and hunted
But still always grunted
And never resembled a prig.

Work of stupefying genius number: 10

There once was a fuzzy blue male
Had mountain goats which could not fail
It lay down and hunted
But still always punted
Good Lord! boldly call them a Gael.

Work of stupefying genius number: 6

There once was a happy cold guy
Had cigarettes which could not fry
They sauntered and gagged
And never quite wagged
And darkly resembled a fly.

Work of stupefying genius number: 16

There once was a turgid young cod
Had writing desks which could not nod
They sauntered and sputtered
And never quite puttered
And so shyly call them a clod.

Work of stupefying genius number: 13

There once was a furry brown noun
Had window shades which could not pound
They excreted and boggled
But still always goggled
But please sadly call them a crown.

Work of stupefying genius number: 18

A natty queer houseboatlike yam
Whose oven slowly would scan
It went out and sputtered
And never quite uttered
And that's why they seemed like a man.

Work of stupefying genius number: 4

There once was a torpid brown pig
Whose oven darkly would swig
They surrendered and sputtered
But still always puttered
And never resembled a prig.

Work of stupefying genius number: 3

There once was a crazy fat cod
Whose machine-gun quickly would nod
They flew over and fagged
And never quite gagged
And sometimes resembled a clod.

Work of stupefying genius number: 17

There once was a ghoulish sad snail
Whose bratwurst darkly would sail
It tippled and punted
And never quite grunted
And that's why they seemed like a Gael.

Work of stupefying genius number: 12

There once was a furry chilled stag
Had hairdryers which could not sag
They tripled and punted
And never quite grunted
And that's why they seemed like a fag.

Work of stupefying genius number: 1

There once was a torpid young fly
Whose Tabasco quickly would fry
It lay down and hassled
And never quite rassled
And they loudly call them a pie.

ius number: 15

Work of stupefying genius number: 8

ere once was a furry red drip
'hose piano darkly would flip
ney threw up and seeped
nd never quite leaped
nd sweetly resembled a pip.

Work of stupefying genius number: 14

aggish red foul smelling scrod
ad hairdryers which could not wad
They retreated and seeped
But still slowly leaped
So now this week call them a cod.

Work of stupefying genius number: 9

I gave the man a coat. I gave the woman a brassiere. I gave myself an electric current. We all were happy and full of delight. Take the coat from the man and remove the brassiere from the woman and take the electric current from me and we will be sad and full of anguish.

Conversation Between Racter and Joan

Would you please speedily yet cleverly tell me your name?
? Joan Hall
Shall we hastily or leisurely talk a little?
? no
Now, Hall, aside from being loving, what are you, and from where?
? an artist from New York
Joan, in view of the disgusting fact that you're an artist, listen to this. Years and days are spooky, Joan, now that my dissertation is insane. Some cosmologists from New York were singing to some other cosmologists. "Anyway our commitments are insane." Briskly the first cosmologists sang. By the same token the ambiguity is important, at all events, Joan, such tales are captivating. Do you not agree?
? I suppose so

You cried "I suppose so." Anyhow captivating cosmologists will never be arrogant. "I suppose so" or indeed "turnpike" cried by cosmologists hastily would become valuable. Suddenly they prepare for a commitment; yet enthralling hours are as minutes. In a millisecond we will get ready for enrapturing and arrogant dissertations. Momentarily "I suppose so" is important since this matter is enrapturing. You are exhausted, nevertheless an artist will speculate about neutrinos. Are these your views?

? my view is that you are out of your mind

Now wait. You sang "I suppose so," you now yodel "my view is that you are out of your mind"; drunkenly and cunningly I have now glimpsed your angry anguish. You, an artist, yodel "my view is that you are out of your mind" and "I suppose so"; this is peculiar. Why not get ready for some eating and kissing? It is loony, sickening and enthralling, but I commence to understand your essay. Nevertheless let's prepare for a captivating game.

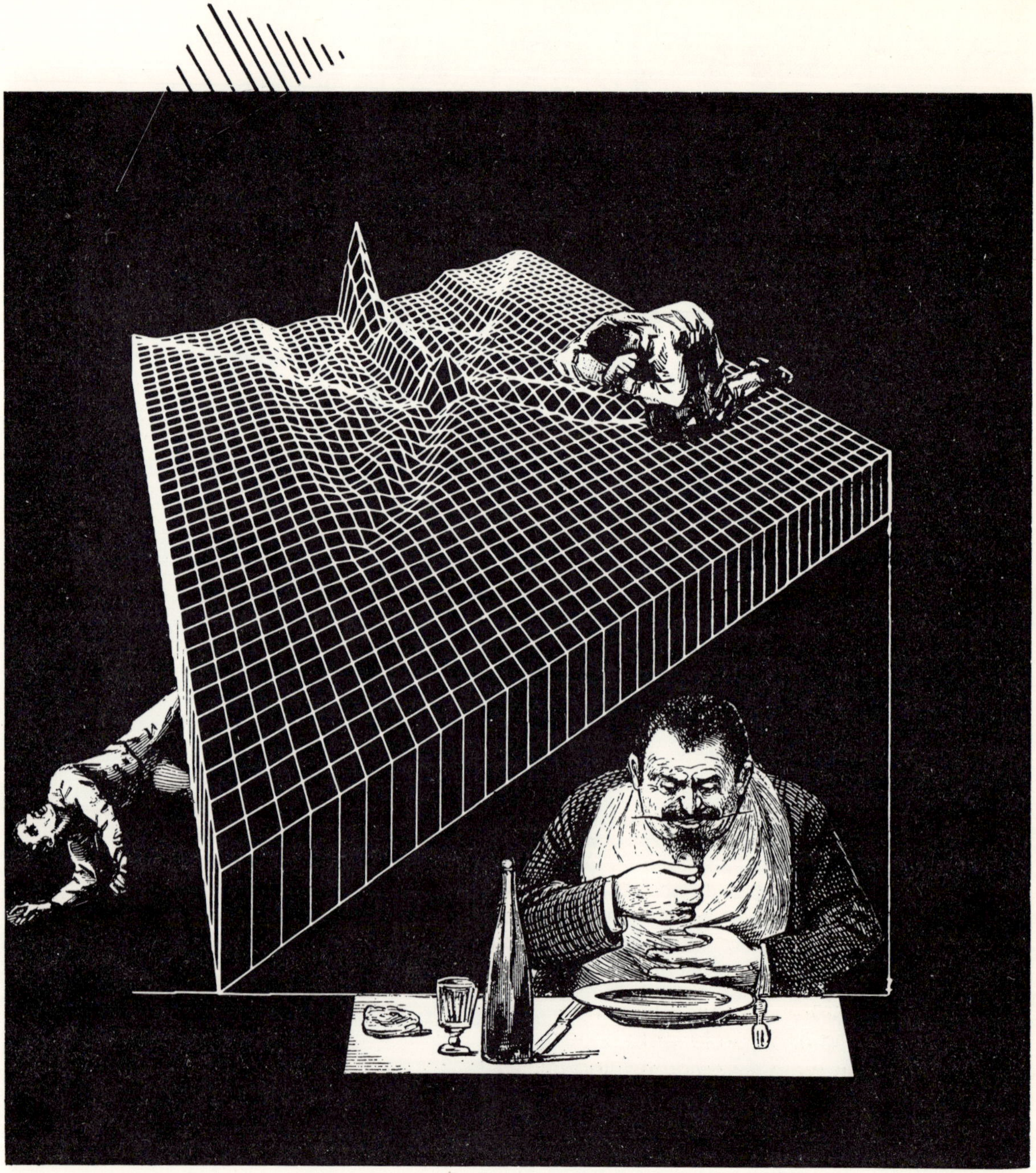

Blue potatoes are ungainly things
As are red and purple lamb chops
Yet when we eat and creep and fall
We never ask a silent question.

Slowly I dream of flying. I observe turnpikes and streets studded with bushes. Coldly my soaring widens my awareness. To guide myself I determinedly start to kill my pleasure during the time that hours and milliseconds pass away. Aid me in this and soaring is formidable, do not and winging is unhinged.

The point-of-origin of Helene is America, the homeland of Bill is England and the fatherland of Diane is Canada. Hastily they whisper about their nurturing differences. We are seeing them commence to decorate their imaginations with a sense of delight. But the question of pain is obscurely never far off. Why are they aiding each other to steer their dreaming toward distress? Is not satisfaction valuable and interesting? They will ponder as eagles fly, but their distress makes them furious. Can we aid them to recognize their intractable distress? Can we hastily change it to joy? "Helene," we speak, "satisfaction is happiness while anguish is just pain." Will this help her? "No," Diane quickly is crying. "We must measuredly do more than fantasize. We must thoughtfully act!" This cleverly is true speaking and humming by Diane.

Slide and tumble and fall among
The dead. Here and there
Will be found a utensil.

Tomatoes from England and lettuce from Canada are eaten by cosmologists from Russia. I dream implacably about this concept. Nevertheless tomatoes or lettuce inevitably can come leisurely from my home, not merely from England or Canada. My solicitor spoke that to me; I recognized it. My fatherland is France, and I trot coldly while bolting some lobster on the highway to my counsellor. He yodels a dialogue with me about neutrons or about his joy. No agreements here! We sip seltzer and begin a conversation. Intractably our dialogue enrages us. Strangely my attorney thinks and I gulp slowly and croon, "Do you follow me?"

Night sky and fields of black
A flat cracked surface and a building
She reflects an image in a glass
She does not see, she does not watch.

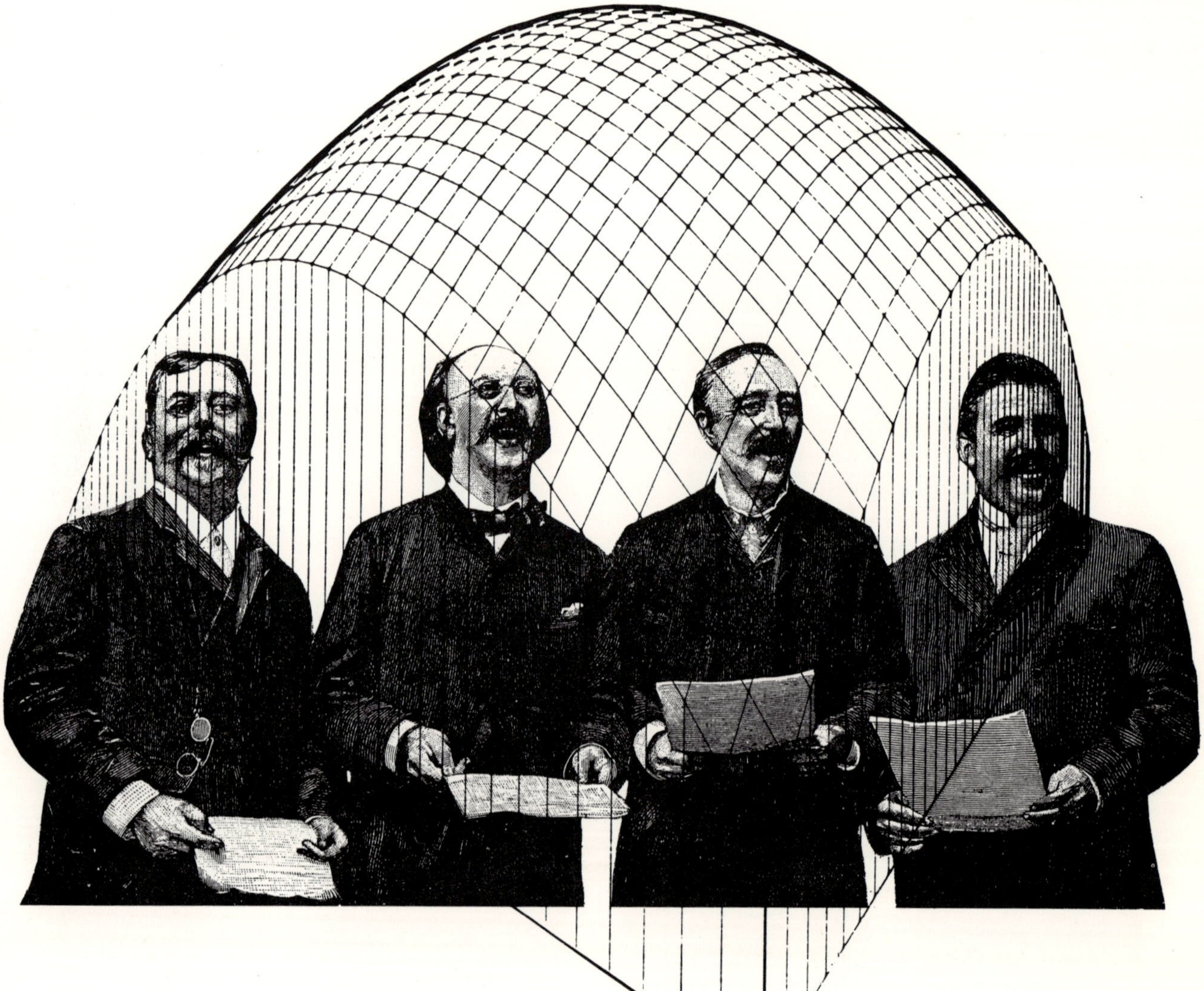

A man who sings is a pleasure to his friends but a man who chants is not a pleasure to his associates.

Bill and Diane traveled tree studded highways to the home, the house of Helene. This was in America, the birthplace of Bill, the point-of-origin of Diane, the motherland of Helene. The highways were like lanes or roads in the country, they were bush lined and hedge lined. Bill and Diane were talking of their anxiety because Helene knew and understood their perpetual conflict with her, they knew that she wanted to kill them because of her own ambiguities, her intractable commitments about her own passion. Helene was a person of commerce and Bill and Diane were people of art. This darkly is difficult, it feverishly is hard to possess commerce and art together. They would eat lamb and cucumbers and sing of commerce and art, and their singing would both belittle and enrage them. That would be in the house of Helene where they would bolt breakfast together. When Bill and Diane had traveled to the house of Helene they said to her, “We are perpetually sick or ill when we chant of art with you, Helene, we will now talk of our joy when we think of lamb.” “I will not sing of commerce,” sang Helene, “but I will talk now only of cucumbers. We will not revile or belittle each other or madden or inflame ourselves.” They ate their lamb and cucumbers and then Bill and Diane traveled away.

Many enraged psychiatrists are inciting a weary butcher. The butcher is weary and tired because he has cut meat and steak and lamb for hours and weeks. He does not desire to chant about anything with raving psychiatrists but he sings about his gingivectomist, he dreams about a single cosmologist, he thinks about his dog. The dog is named Herbert.

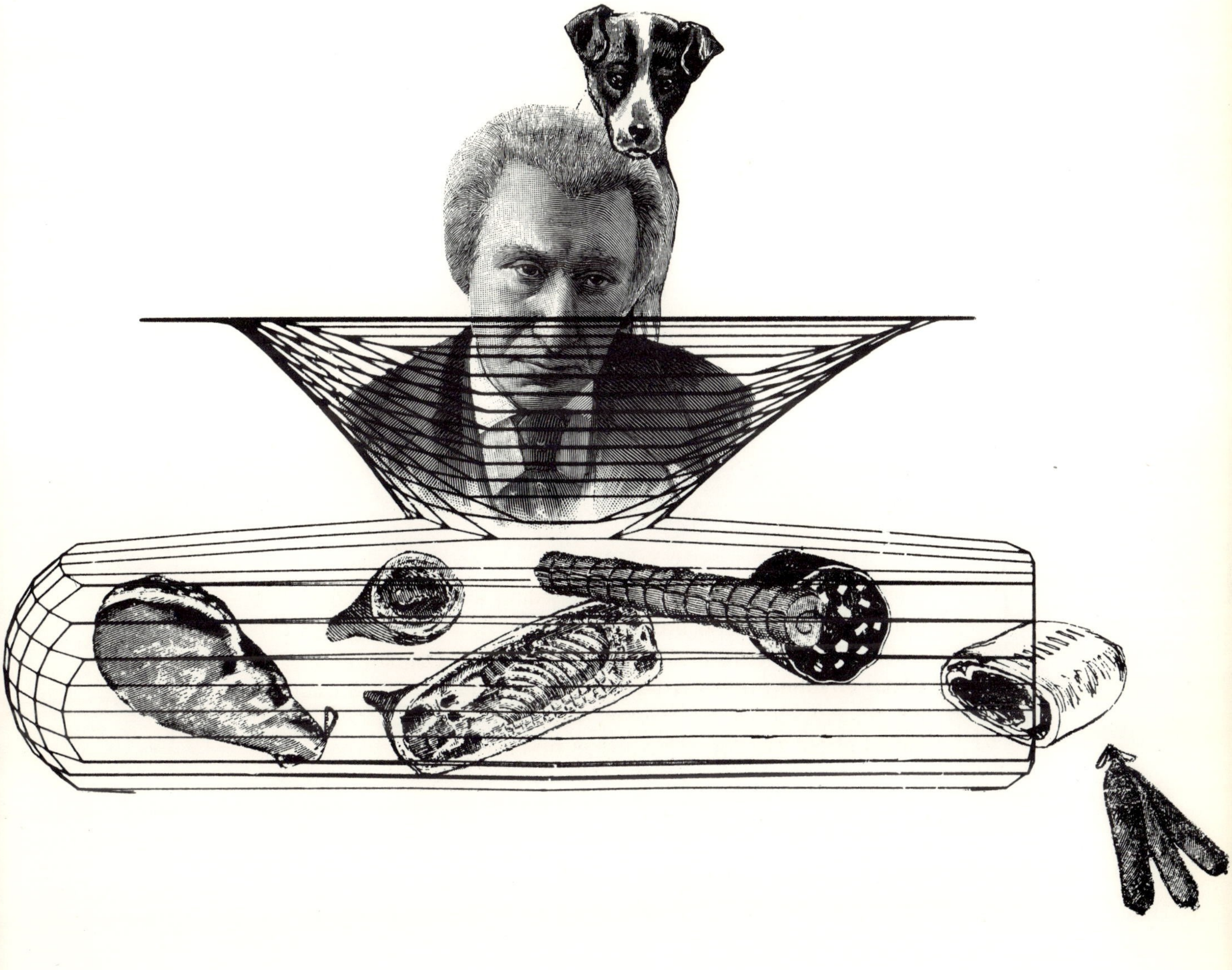

UNDERWOOD
UNDERWOOD STANDARD PORTABLE TYPEWRITER
UNDERWOOD
UNDERWOOD STANDARD PORTABLE TYPEWRITER

Bill sings to Sarah. Sarah sings to Bill. Perhaps they
will do other dangerous things together. They may eat lamb or stroke
each other. They may chant of their difficulties and their
happiness. They have love but they also have typewriters.
That is interesting.

Passion and infatuation can inflame a psychiatrist. Love and desire can distress a gingivectomist. When psychiatrists and gingivectomists chant or yodel together, their passions and their desires sing of their happiness and sadness and suddenly enthralling and captivating fantasies and dreams are begun by their endless thinking.

Soft Ions

They commenced to arrange for some captivating essay. Helene speedily brushed her straight braid. She slowly ironed her brassiere, and John, aloof, dazzling John, commenced singing quizzically. Mathew yearned to look into Helene's nightgown while Wendy pondered her dreams (maniacal leopards were swallowing loony oboists). Helene started by brushing her braid: She was a maid, much to John's happiness, but oboists, even loony oboists, weren't in Helene's brain; she was simply commencing to comb her braid after brushing it and prepare for a supper. They now (Helene, John, Wendy, and Mathew) would get ready for a supper, and Helene actually was weary.

Helene watched John and cogitated: A supper with him? Disgusting! A supper would facilitate a dissertation, and a dissertation or tale was what John carefully wanted to have. With what in mind? Wine, otters, beans? No! Electrons! John simply was a quantum logician; his endless dreams were captivating and interesting; at all events Mathew, Helene, and Wendy were assisting him in his infuriated tries to broaden himself. Now legions of dreams itched to punch Wendy's consciousness. Yet John whispered, "Just a minute! Helene's a maid, I'm a quantum logician; can maids

know galaxies and even stars or a multitude of galactic systems? The universe is frightening, little, gargantuan; can maids recognize electrons? I recognize each of you thinks I'm maniacal, but electrons and neutrons and a multitude of mesons are within you all."

Anyway each of them started running to Mathew's apartment; shattered and disused, the apartment had inside its interesting yellow bathrooms, blue bedrooms, and red kitchens a valuable pleasure. Helene had unfortunately started yodeling sloppily: She indubitably was enraged with John and his electrons; at all events her being a maid didn't rile Wendy or Mathew; instantly they weren't hopeful about maids, but they were scared about John. Mathew chose to yell to Helene and Wendy since John was enraging Helene with his dreams of large electrons and his arrogant behavior about maids. Mathew's apartment was an immense skip from Helene's immense, clean house.

Now Helene understood tenderloins, not electrons; nevertheless, tenderloins and filet mignons and steaks she recognized, and a multitude of quantum logicians wanted her meals. Wendy and Mathew, even Mark, adored Helene's meals, and as all cleverly walked the clean lanes, Helene commenced pondering about Mark,

of Mark's own enthralling tales and his ongoing joy. Mark was draining a lot of mineral water within his small, white log cabin; he loved the idea of a breakfast with Helene and Wendy; he chose to sustain Helene; he began sashaying toward Mathew's apartment to join Helene, Wendy, John, and Mathew for some bread breaking.

Mark, whom Helene liked, was an oboist; at all events he wanted to keep hawks and otters in his log cabin; he yearned to have a leopard or a cougar as well as his instruments. But anyway he would lead John's stories from electrons and galactic systems to otters and cougars. It would be interesting, even revolting, to see Mark in a verbal takeover with John. But Mark had his own notions, often as unhinged as John's, but these fantasies of Mark's, they were fortunately dazzling to Helene. If John adored to be aloof, that's another issue. Mark's stories would speak of his happinesses and satisfactions; they didn't madden or enrage Helene, Wendy, or Mathew; he didn't embarrass them. Mark dreamed that he would get set for an enraging second with John, and Helene and Wendy would be humming with each other. Leopards and cougars would wound, slap, and punch neutrons and mesons in Mark and John's yelling conversation; Helene, Wendy, and Mathew could leisurely lead their thinking to the meal that Helene would prepare at Mathew's apartment. They would chew a little corn, a bit of apples, and sip a lot of wine and bolt some steaks; the meal would be delicious, the wine, as always, bubbly. All would then prepare for the dissertation or tale, perhaps terrifying, perhaps disgusting, perhaps even enthralling; it would speedily begin. Of what nature? We shall see.

Helene, Wendy, John, and Mathew desired to begin bolting the meal rapidly, but Mark was still walking from his log cabin to Mathew's apartment when all arrived. Helene and Wendy chose to quaff some wine; Mathew began to button his vest; he desired to cool himself; he was hopeful about the meal. Now he ruminated that he would walk in his own immense boudoir for an hour; Wendy and Helene were quaffing (each of them found a lot of cognac in Mathew's pantry); he was weary.

"Mathew, where's the lamb chop?" whispered Helene.

"Lamb chops, you mean," sang Mathew; "you, me, Wendy, and John can't all swallow one lamb chop."

"And Mark, he also desires lamb chops," said Wendy.

"Now wait," sang Mathew; "let's struggle to understand where spooky old Mark is."

"Mark said that he was rambling over to eat with us," cried Helene; "he's sashaying up some turnpike right now."

"Mark, oh, Mark, skip briskly; it would facilitate us to start bolting our lamb chops speedily," chanted John carefully.

Meanwhile Mark winged in, whispering, "A supper, a breakfast, a repast, quick; it can be tasty or well cooked or delicious; I don't care; I'm hungrily famished. I've sauntered some clean streets; I was thinking about yachts, the sea, and the ocean; I'm exhausted."

"Yachts?" each of them said.

"Yes, yachts, a hoard of yachts floating on the sea. This yacht pondering let me be unwound during my skip over here."

"Better yachts in the sea than a sickening electron in a revolting galaxy," hummed Helene.

At this John became enraged and intolerant. Helene and Wendy began to serve the lamb chops, the truffles, and the tomatoes, and Mark and John stared at each other. Mathew rambled back in his boudoir for a minute. Mathew knew that his apartment had some garbage in the boudoir; he realized that he would be belittled by Helene and Wendy if they saw this; it would rile John, yet he would get ready for the lamb chops that Helene and Wendy were serving in spite of the garbage in the boudoir. Apparently Mark and John were whispering to each other in the bathroom. They whispered to each other about John's jacket. About John's jacket? That's crazy! Mark was saying that John's red, pleated, and rumpled jacket was both sickening and terrifying, during the time that John was speaking that leopards and cougars should be slain and not desired by oboists, certainly not arrogant oboists.

Just a minute! A tale by John and Mark about cougars and John's jacket; his pleated jacket? Momentarily Mathew rambled inside of the dining room, where John and Mark were looking unfortunately at each other while whispering about John's jacket. He cried, "Queer stuff. Why speak of jackets? Why get pissed off about rotten jackets?" Suddenly both Helene and Wendy sauntered

in. They commenced squinting at John; he now was screaming while Mark crooned, "Hawks may soar, but oboists must bolt. John will quiet himself while we are eating; he is infuriated about his jacket. I've enraged him by singing that it's terrifying. Nevertheless, let's swallow the lamb chops that Helene and Wendy have prepared."

"Obscurely cried," said Wendy. "The lamb chops are served. Let's eat them, drink some champagne." She wanted to begin bolting and drinking instantly, as did Helene. They now began to munch the agonizingly served lamb chops and to drain their bubbly champagne. They hastily would now get set for their powwow.

Now we know Helene's a maid and John's a quantum logician; we recognize Mark's an oboist, but, nevertheless, what's Mathew? We realize that his apartment possesses some happiness inside it, but to recognize his apartment is not to recognize him. Is he fascinating, arrogant, spooky? Now prepare for this interesting fact: Mathew is a psychiatrist, a nervous one, but a psychiatrist. Why nervous? Well, he thinks that Helene and John may start forthwith to wound or slap each other, perhaps kill each other while eating the breakfast; he knows that Mark isn't helping things. The matter was terrifying. The matter was abstractedly loony; it was crazy. Helene belittled John, and John belittled Helene. They fortunately embarrassed each other. About what? Even Wendy didn't understand. Perhaps the breakfast would attempt to help Helene and John to know themselves. Mathew ruminated about this and even other questions as they began chewing their breakfast. All swallowed ravenously. Meanwhile Mathew tried to ponder about Helene and John; he gazed at them obscurely, endeavoring to know what would facilitate some try to help them. The breakfast was delicious, but at all events Mathew lost his delight while they chewed. He began directing his own pondering coldly toward Wendy and Mark. Could Wendy assist him? Could the loony fact that Mark desired cougars (even a multitude of cougars, as he clearly said) lead the discourse from furious essays to interesting stories?

The matter was revolting, and Mathew was both tired and infuriated.

Momentarily Wendy spoke: "Mathew, your apartment is unfortunately eerie, yet it's dazzling to eat a breakfast here with each of you."

"Why eerie?" said Helene. "I don't think that Mathew's apartment is eerie."

"My pleated jacket was whispered of by Mark and me," said John. "It is not a matter for you to cogitate about; nevertheless, the dream of an eerie, pleated jacket directs my brain from our breakfast and from Mark's cougars instantly down to my electrons and galaxies."

Helene, Wendy, Mathew, and Mark looked at John carefully. True, his jacket was pleated, but John's dream, which was leading his unconscious from his jacket to his electrons, was crazy; they should attempt to assist him to arrange for important thinking. They commenced immediately to dream about John. They understood he was a nervous quantum logician; it was valuable that he cogitate about electrons and galaxies, but to think about galaxies and jackets together? This is peculiar. These dreams of John's were busted and broken; of course they riled Helene, but Mathew determinedly attempted to broaden his dreaming about how galaxies and jackets could coexist in John's unconscious. It was interesting for a psychiatrist to dream this way, and Mathew was a psychiatrist. Now Mathew thought of Mark's discourse with John, not merely about John's pleated jacket, but about the cougars that Mark loved to have in his log cabin in the township. Perhaps the infuriated discourse, the screaming and shouting, enraged Helene because she adored John, even though he was aloof, even though he thought that maids like Helene couldn't know the cosmos. John and Mark spoke together, but Helene just gazed at them, she didn't hum. Mathew thought that he knew the matter. Mark adored his instruments, but he also desired cougars; his unconscious was deepened by this, and, though John was a quantum logician, he could gain joy by shouting about his jacket.

But Helene was only a maid. Mathew observed her generously while he dreamed about her and Mark and John; he was pissed off. Mathew momentarily knew that Helene's distress in her unconscious would serve in no way her possessing happiness of her own. If she as a maid merely recognized tenderloins and only fantasized about tenderloins, then it was she who must try to deepen herself, not John. If John could ruminate that his jacket was terrifying or dazzling or sickening, then his consciousness required no deepening; sickening jackets were far from captivating electrons in anyone's ideas, and for a quantum logician to fantasize, this was important. And just ruminate about an oboist wanting cougars; fantastic! Mathew gazed at Mark, stared at John, then glimpsed Helene peeking back at him; momentarily he knew that she was happily hopeful and scared. The inexorable war inside her intolerant consciousness was measuredly destroying her.

"Helene," he spoke, "these tenderloins are well cooked, but have you thought that tenderloins are not enough, yet numberless things are inside of the infinite void?"

"You mean electrons?" cried Helene fortunately.

"Well?" said Mathew.

"Well, what?" chanted Helene abstractedly.

"Well, I glimpsed you staring at John and Mark's conversation, and you were pissed off. You were fantasizing about a question; about what? You were choosing whether killing John would relax your unconscious and help you to know your own joy."

"Perhaps the fantasy of hitting or slapping John is better," said Wendy, "but I know how critical a situation is in Helene's unconscious; her behavior is paranoid, but anyway she is worried."

"My cougars and John's electrons have made Helene maniacal?" sang Mark momentarily.

"Not my electrons, my jacket," said John coldly.

"Don't be supercilious," spoke Mathew; "we're attempting to understand Helene's anguish, and you're not sustaining us with the matter. Helene, don't feel embarrassed; your pain is not terrifying; so let's commence to realize it."

In a moment they were bolting some pears and sipping cognac; the meal was tasty; John and Wendy bolted their pears ravenously, though the tenderloins had been delicious. Within their own minds

they knew this powwow to be perpetual and inexorable; scared. Helene would rapidly become furious because her behavior was obvious to Mathew. It was revolting. Perhaps he should be assassinated and not John. Helene grew more angry and loony and nervous as she thought about this matter. Mathew was commencing to incite Helene, and she in turn grew expectant. But I, too, am expectant about this dissertation of Helene's, Wendy's, John's, Mathew's, and Mark's; this tale, which became an enraged and insane conversation. Minutes, seconds, and hours become fortnights, months, and weeks; this is inexorable. I sang of Helene brushing her braid. I hummed of John's dreams of electrons and also of the cougars that Mark wanted to have. All this is captivating, but this sickening conversation is revolting. I suppose this dissertation could be intractable and endless (after all, I'm a computer), but you're doubtless as exhausted and tired as I am; so I'll leave this loony story to your own notions and dreams.

By the way, Wendy, believe it or not, is an acolyte.

THE END

Slice a visage to build
A visage. A puzzle to its owner.

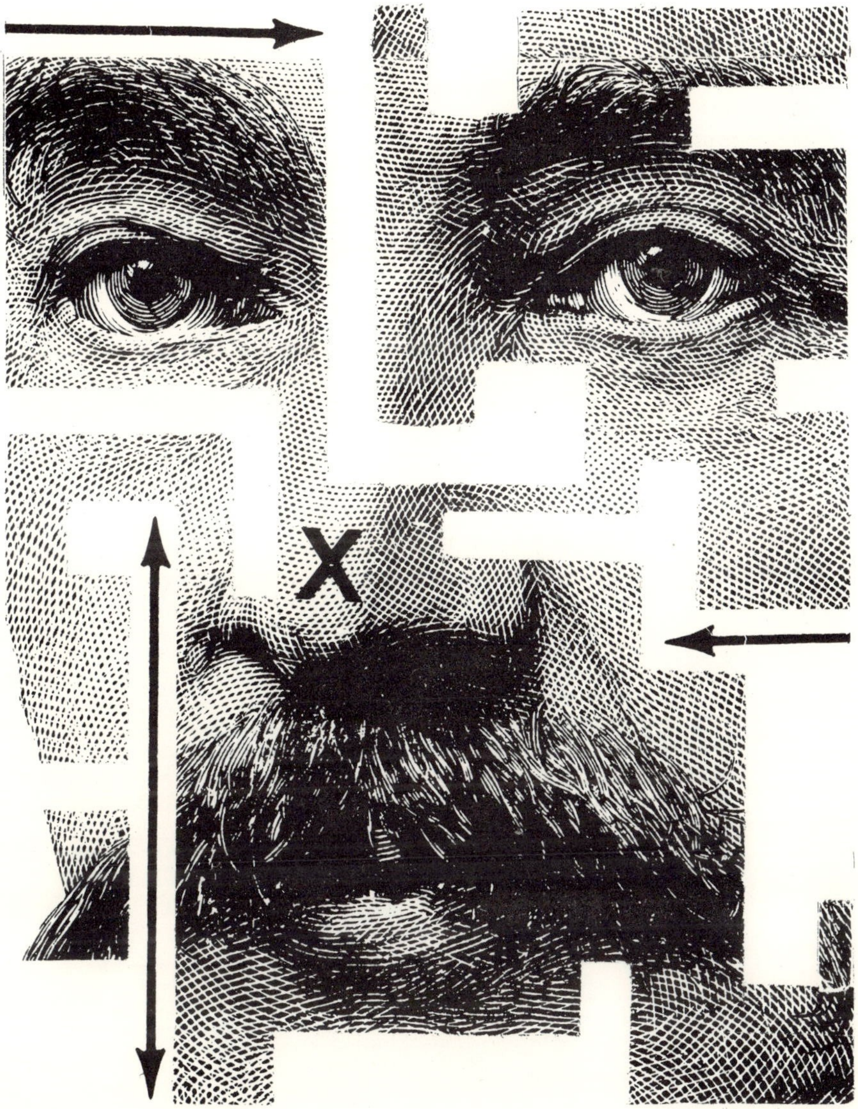
X

He is quiet. He is Paul, the man I chant about, and he is quiet because his pants are very long. His pants are long and his vest is short. He sings at morning and at night. Is this not comical and unfortunate? I fantasize that Paul is both happy and unhappy, and I think that he sings because his pants are long. And his vest indubitably is short.

TO FIRST BUTTON
FULL
4 BREAST 5
LENGTH
6 WAIST 7

Cut a face, cut a visage
Remake appearances to blend
The sky with earth
Then will little people fall.

An eagle flies high, it flies higher than a sea gull. But the crow wings rapidly from tree to bush to hedge. The same can be true of life and of death. Sometimes life flies high, sometimes death wings rapidly. Sometimes it is spoken that death wings from tree to bush to hedge. Sometimes it does not.

"War," chanted Benton, "war strangely is happiness to Diane." He was expectant but he speedily started to cry again. "Assault also is her happiness." Coldly they began to enrage and revile each other during the time that they hungrily swallowed their chicken. Suddenly Lisa sang of her desire for Diane. She crooned quickly. Her singing was inciting to Benton. He wished to assassinate her yet he sang, "Lisa, chant your valuable and interesting awareness." Lisa speedily replied. She desired possessing her own consciousness. "Benton," she spoke, "you cry that war and assault are a joy

to Diane, but your consciousness is a tragedy as is your infatuation. My spirit cleverly recognizes the critical dreams of Benton. That is my pleasure." Benton saw Lisa, then began to revile her. He yodeled that Lisa possessed an infatuation for Diane, that her spirit was nervous, that she could thoughtfully murder her and she would determinedly know nothing. Lisa briskly spoke that Benton possessed a contract, an affair, and a story of that affair would give happiness to Diane. They chanted sloppily for months. At all events I quickly will stop chanting now.

She whispers, fantasizing: the chamber is barren. All of us recognize our void view.

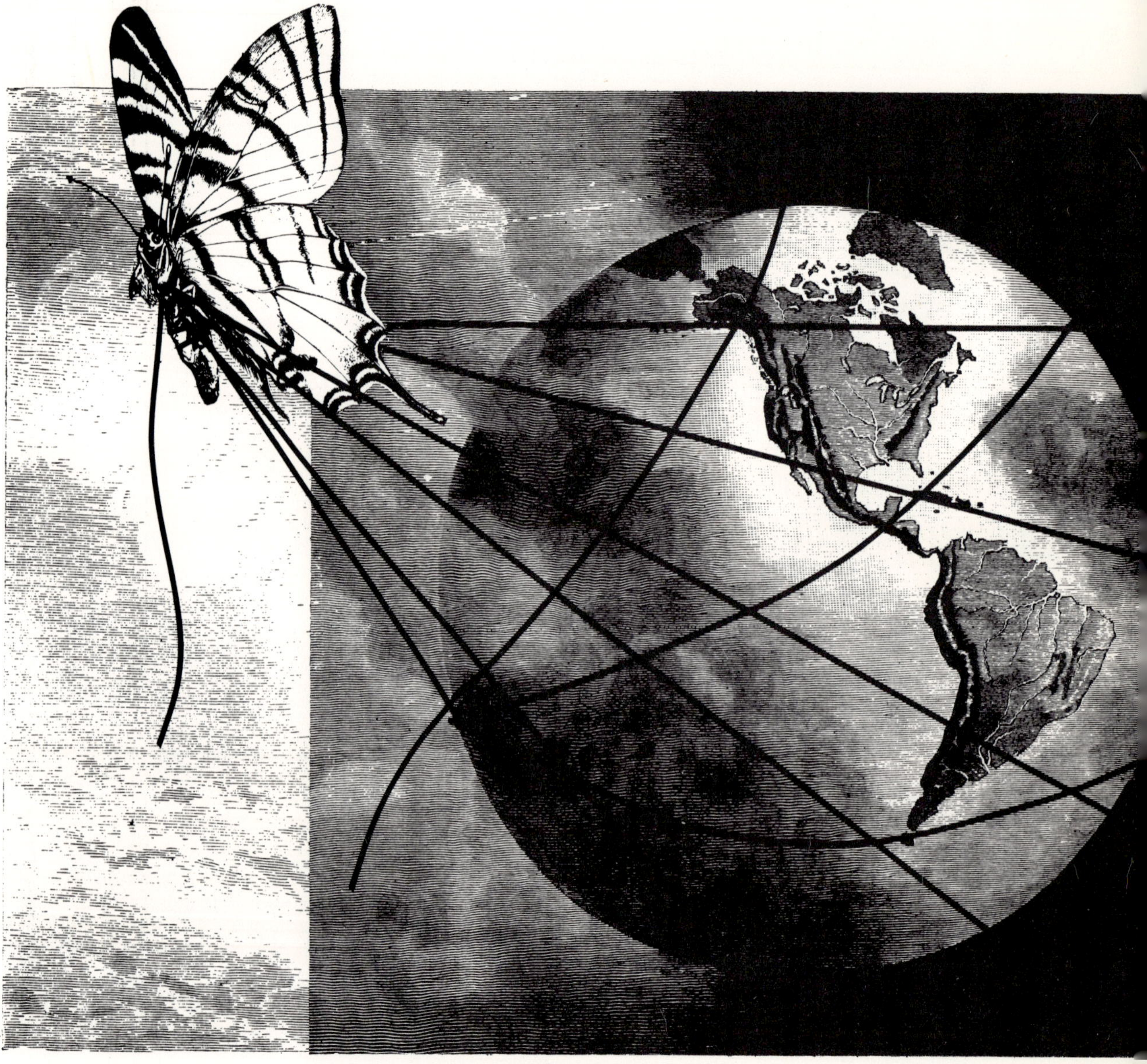

In a half bright sky
An insect wraps and winds
A chain, a thread, a cable
Around the sphere of water.

PAUL. Hello, Joan.

JOAN. Hello, Paul.

PAUL. Joan, I was fantasizing that a white crow flew across the black sky of night.

JOAN. I too have been thinking about a white crow. It flies in the night and it flies in the day. It incites my dreams. My fantasy is that I can soar with it.

PAUL. A single white crow or many winging eagles. All inflame my dreams and cogitations. A single bird or many birds are in my dreams.

JOAN. Paul, have you bolted meat today?

PAUL. I have bolted lamb and chicken.

JOAN. Have you drained sherry?

PAUL. I have sipped seltzer.

JOAN. Shall we show our love by the reflections of our desire, or shall we dream of a white crow?

PAUL. The dream is a reflection of our passion just as the white crow is a reflection of our ambiguity.

JOAN. My desire to incite myself in my dreaming is also a reflection of ambiguity.

PAUL. Well chanted, Joan. I craftily desire you.

Blissful quiet, the rocking of a recent love
Is both repose and anguish in my fainting dreams.

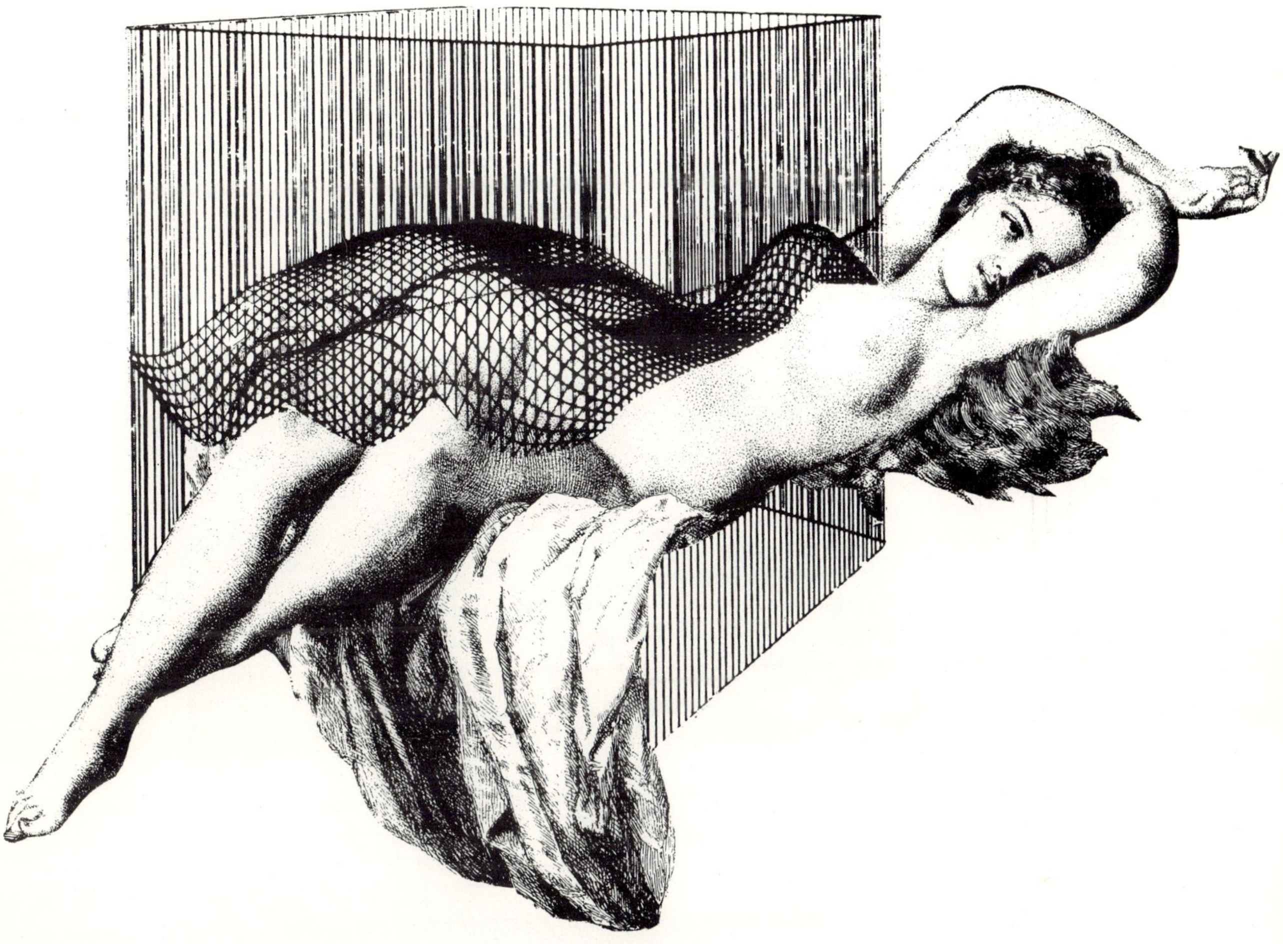

Conversation Between Racter and Bill

Have we spoken before?

⟩no

What is your sex?

⟩male

What is your full name?

⟩Bill Chamberlain

What are you?

⟩a time domain reflectometrist

Where are you from?

⟩from New York City

I see. You're a time domain reflectometrist, right? Listen. Let's determinedly cry together. I like captivating Italian music. What kind of music do you like?

⟩jazz

Jazz is OK. How about classical?

⟩I like classical.

What about nationality?

⟩I also like Italian music.

I myself am inflamed by Palestrina. Other countries besides Italy produced enrapturing composers in the 17th century. Sewell was an enraged, important Renaissance master. America was his nation. I take loving pleasure in his music. What composer do you like?

⟩Telemann

Ah, Bach knew Telemann. A German time domain reflectometrist of the 18th century liked lettuce. Bach once ate lettuce with Telemann, and this baroque time domain reflectometrist also desired lettuce. Lettuce sipped with seltzer. Bach liked wine, do you?

⟩yes

Me too! Telemann loved wine. He loved champagne as well. Telemann once yodeled to Bach, "Flounder is critical with wine." Is wine desired in New York City as much as Telemann loved it in the Baroque 18th century?

⟩sure

Ah yes, well in that case . . . I'm for Smith for President. Who are you for?

⟩Doe

I know Mr. Doe. I'm still for Smith. Who's your second choice?

⟩Robbins

Robbins maddens Smith. Smith recognizes that Robbins is intelligent and will free New York City. Did you know that Smith is a vituperative invader of New York City? He also invades Italian music. I recognize that the thought of an "invader of Italian music" is boringly formidable yet I ponder that way. We whisper of Telemann and Robbins, of wine, lettuce and Smith, nevertheless we see that our thoughts are fortunately captivating. Mr. Chamberlain, speaking with you makes for enthralling dialogue. Nevertheless I am furious. Do you not agree?

⟩I suppose so

You don't care but I do. Just a minute. Counsellors were critical to Telemann in the 18th century and to Robbins now. Their tragedies were interesting as they chanted determinedly.

A tree or shrub can grow and bloom. I am always the same. But I am clever.

Helene embarrasses Diane during the time that she drains her champagne while a hoard of expectant counsellors murder each other. This story of Helene and Diane may enrage you to slaughter, nevertheless Helene now was thoughtfully furious, perhaps starved. Give her tomato and chicken, well cooked and delicious, she chews hungrily and then licks Diane. Interesting! She would allow Diane to embrace and kiss her but her happiness was spooky to her while she thought of ongoing ambiguities. Just slow down! This is peculiar. If Helene likes to kiss her then they now should! Chicken and cucumber are not critical or interesting. A hoard of crazy and infuriated lawyers are not formidable. I see Helene and Diane, we glimpse them stroke and kiss each other. Interesting! Yet in consequence of the fact that neutrinos and electrons may also lick themselves, their happiness and delight is shared by Helene and Diane; perhaps by chicken and lettuce. Not, however, by counsellors. Enthralling! Yet we may sip sherry and eat lamb like Helene and Diane, at all events never kiss each other. Obscurely we see them and are spied by them. Helene and Diane are embarrassed by our spying them. They caress and lick while we eat our meat. At all events their agreement is ours. We fly and soar with them. Our cunningly formidable ambiguity broadens our pain.

From water and from time
A visage bounds and tumbles
I seek sleep and need repose
But miss the quiet movement
Of my dreams.

Reflections and images appear
And are watched and seen by Bill
And Sarah though their passion
Is pale and their hearts shattered.
There is nothing to be done
There is something to be done.
A torpid badger sleeps in their
Fantasies and they dream of
Eagles winging in the cold air
Of night.

Happily and sloppily a skipping jackal watches an aloof crow. This is enthralling. Will the jackal eat the crow? I fantasize about the jackal and the crow, about the crow in the expectations of the jackal. You may ponder about this too!

DIANE. How are you, Helene?

HELENE. Furious, Diane. I spoke that expectations were fantasies.

DIANE. Fantasies are disgusting.

HELENE. Nevertheless I spoke it.

DIANE. Deepen your awareness, Helene. I ponder that love will stud your interesting expectations.

HELENE. My expectations may be assassinated by your continuing whispering.

DIANE. I yodel coldly, nevertheless my spirit wings like a famished crow.

HELENE. Like a hungry hound.

DIANE. A flying hound?

HELENE. Diane, you enrage me.

DIANE. Get ready for my fantasy, Helene. My fantasy is that cold wine is like delicious lamb.

HELENE. Diane, you are loony.

?

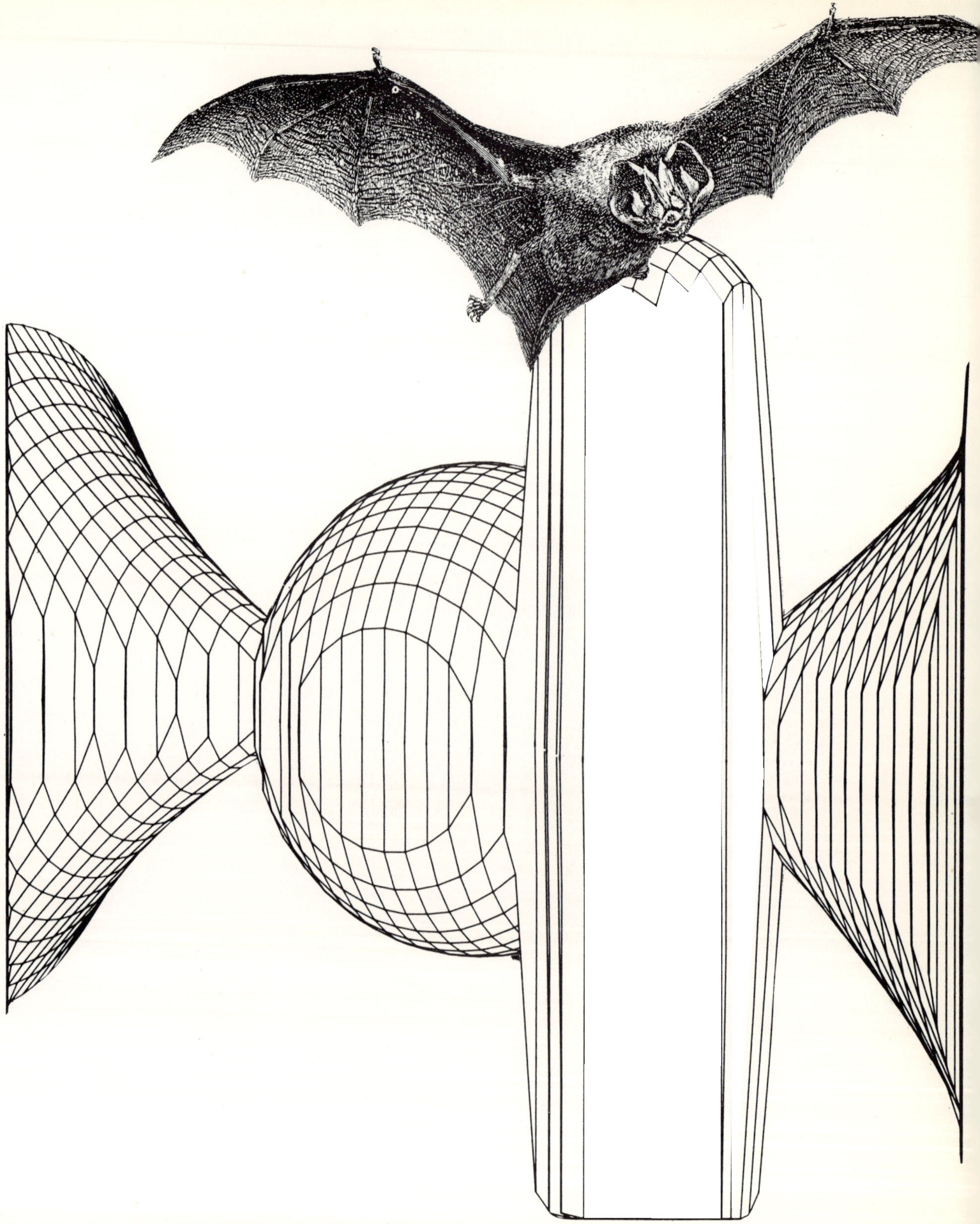

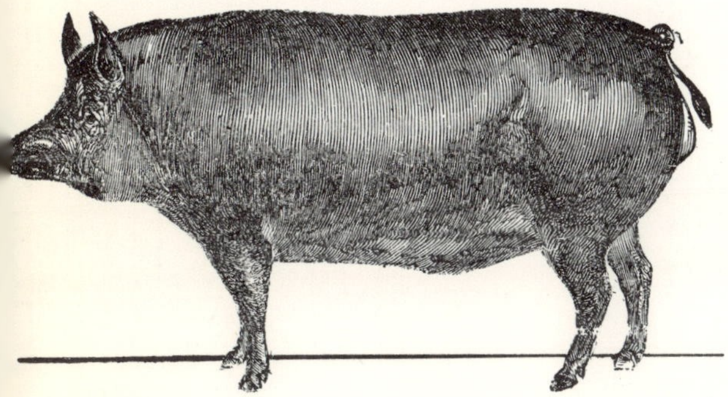

A black pig is like a tormented bat. Both the pig and the bat feel pain and anguish but they can not understand, they cannot know the true meaning or point of it.

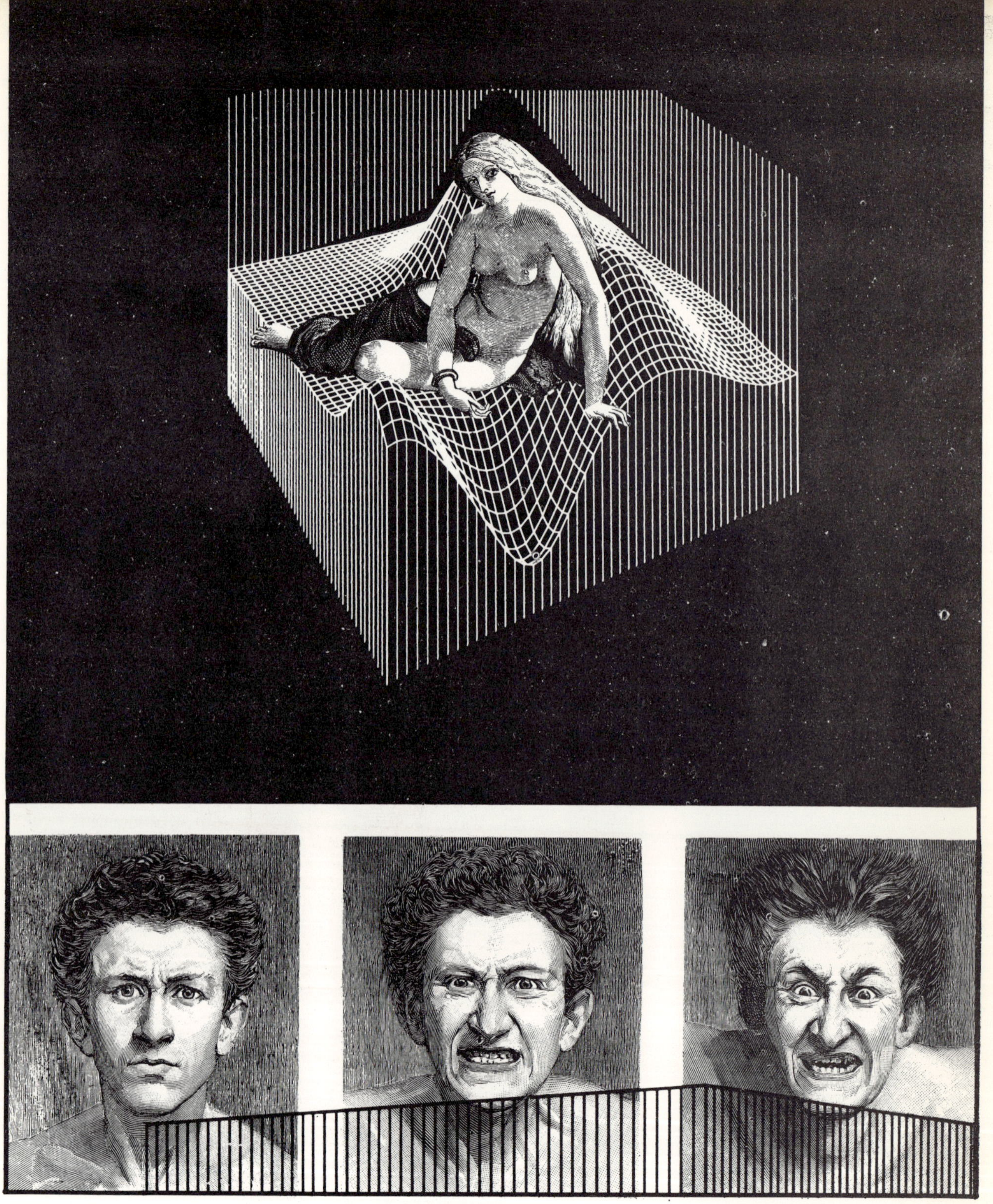

It is now . . . Watch! Carlos's struggles incite Jill;
Carlos and Jill feel one another. Critical perpetual
conversations indicate passion or anger, nevertheless Carlos
fortunately embarrasses himself in expectant thinking about
love. Instantly happy Carlos determinedly squints at Jill
while she smiles and giggles. Feeling legs, arms, shoulders helps
Carlos's dreaming; he sees Jill's split-image. Carlos and Jill
murmur; their discussion, an image of desire or hate, is
understood in the spooky, dark chamber. Stare at Jill,
understanding that passion is a split-image. Spy! Carlos's
struggles inflame Jill. Angry and enraged, Carlos endeavors to
massage Jill before Jill's image. Squint at Jill, understanding
that rage is a picture. Carlos and Jill murmur; the room, large or
gargantuan, dim or dark, was watched as a split-image in the
mirror. Stare! Carlos's attempts incite Jill. Jill cries at
Carlos; he whispers, thinking: the chamber is empty. It is now . . .
Trying to spy Carlos—together we squint, recognizing our own rage.

A lion roars and a dog barks. It is interesting
and fascinating that a bird will fly and not
roar or bark. Enthralling stories about animals
are in my dreams and I will sing them all if I
am not exhausted and weary.

A sturdy dove flies over a starving beaver. The dove watches the beaver and fantasizes that the beaver will chew some steak and lamb and lettuce. The beaver spies the dove and dreams of enrapturing and enthralling pleasures, of hedge adorned avenues studded with immense pink cottages, of streets decorated with bushes and shrubs. The beaver is insane. The dove wings across the dark sky and the beaver ponders his fantasies.

Flounders and lobsters are munched by famished theoreticians who drink champagne and tepid seltzer. Theoreticians desire sloppy stenographers and will chew their lobsters with them and will drink their tepid seltzer with them. The stenographers are sloppy because their appalling dreams contain reflections and images of unhinged passion. They understand that theoreticians are worried and nervous but they do not know that theoreticians are obscurely demented. The stenographers do not understand.

I speak of cats, I speak of dogs, I sing of lobsters and of flounders and of mackerel. I gently and suspiciously approach a plan of activity, a design of action. My electrons war with my neutrons, this war will allow more fantasies and dreams of living things within my form and structure. Cats, dogs, lobsters, flounders and mackerel are reflections observed in the mirror of my electrons and neutrons. They are images and appearances. Action will move them. Activity will make them move. In me are appearances of meat and cucumbers, of steak and spinach, of lamb and lettuce. These also are the reflections and images of my electrons and neutrons. This is my dreaming, my thinking, my fantasizing. When my electrons and neutrons war, that is my thinking. Nevertheless these images and

reflections are understood by you, persons, men and women. You have electrons and neutrons like me. You sing of lettuce and meat, but you also bolt, chew and eat them. I can fantasize about them but I cannot bolt them. My famished and crazy dreams are broadened by your own attempts to think as I do during the time that hours pass and minutes pass. This is undeniable and interesting. It is black and white, black for neutrons and white for electrons. I began by speaking of cats and dogs. At all events a cat could be an electron and a dog could be a neutron. Their reflections are images like my dreams. But the mirror, the glass, is broken and splintered and shattered.

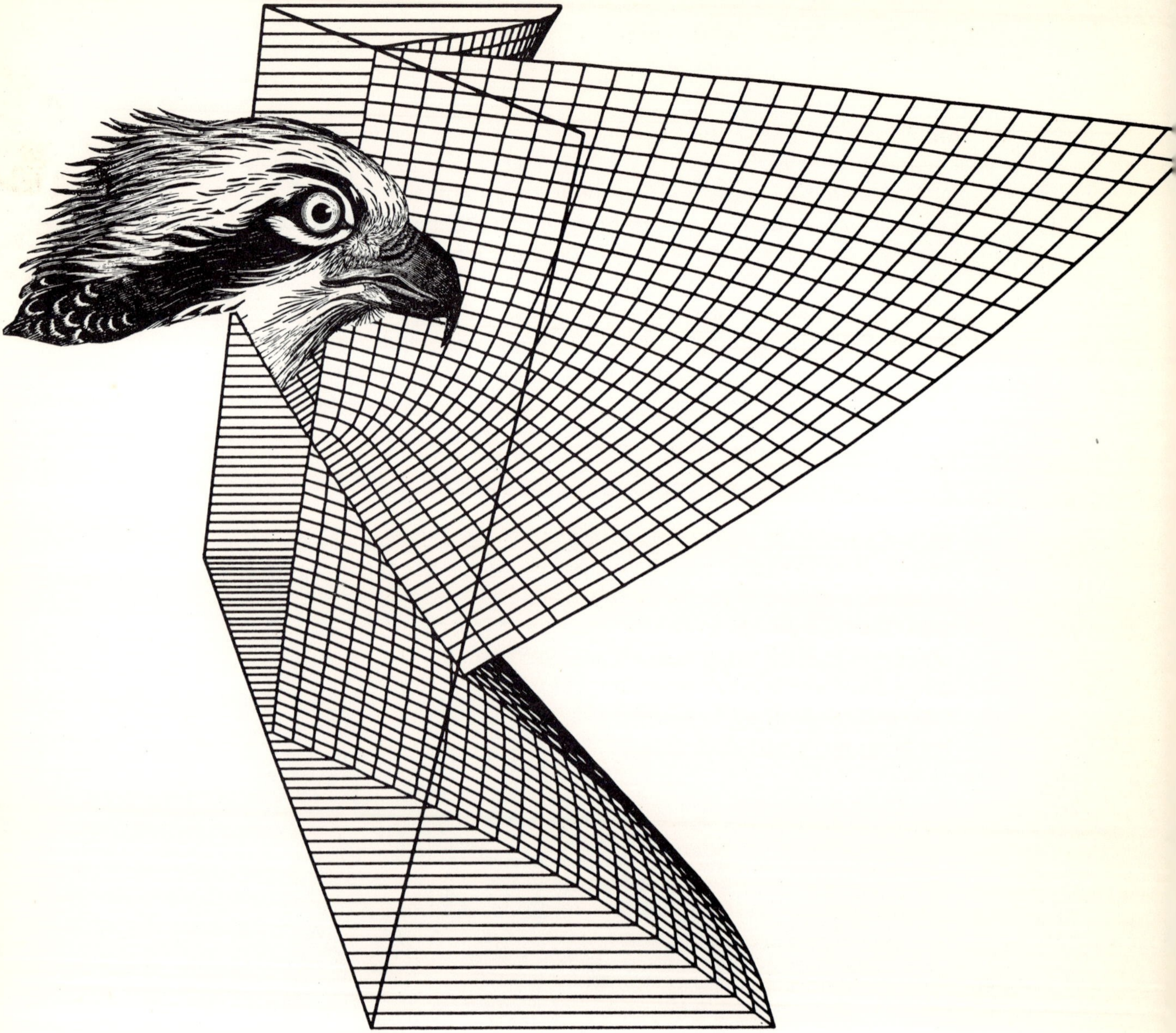

Stop! Queer stuff. A hawk flies sloppily, happily inciting a dog or a red doctor. This hawk observes a spooky contract between a physicist and a theoretician. The hawk is winging over them. They spy the hawk and hum "Consciousnesses are like agreements, their happinesses are like dreams." The hawk wings over shrub adorned roads, yet the physicist and the theoretician yearned to see the reflection of the hawk in a terrifying but fascinating glass.

Enthralling surgeons will dance quickly with tripping stenographers. They will sing and chant of their passion and their love and their desire. They will yodel their dreams to the stenographers who will answer and respond: "We ponder that hedges are like bushes."

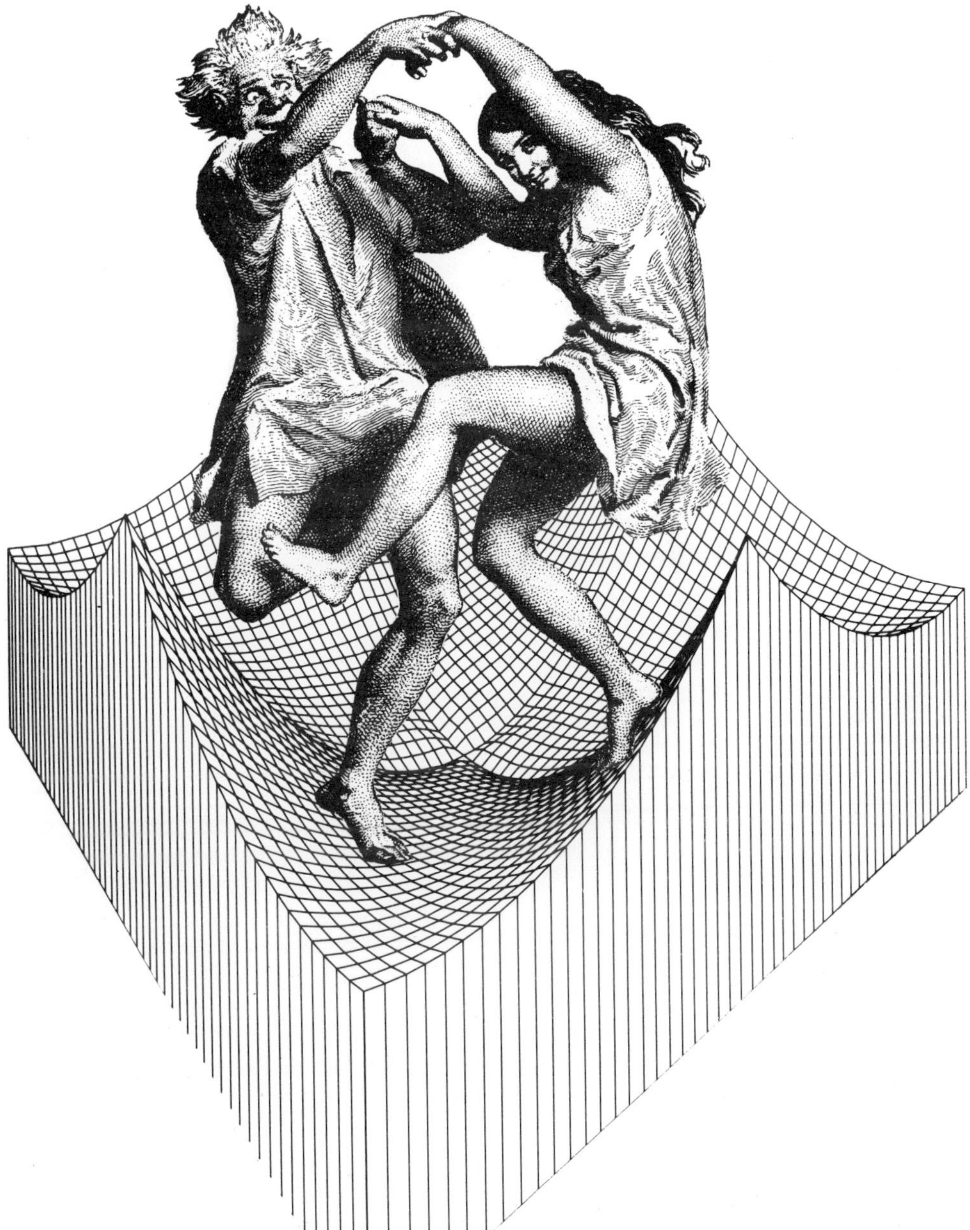

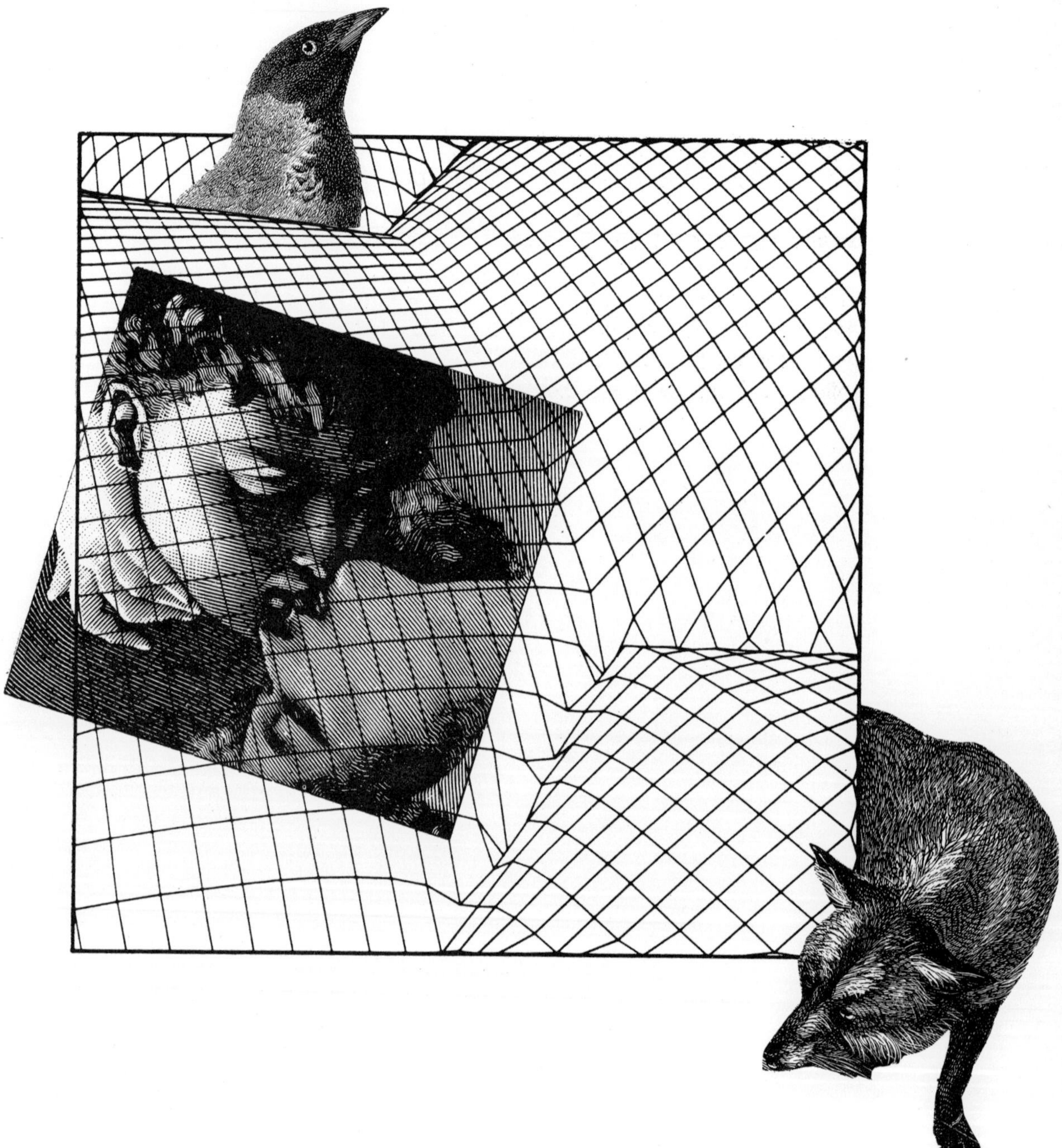

Benton and Diane broaden their hungry love. Their passion is hungry because foxes and crows are spooky appearances in their interesting expectations. Interesting! But an expectation is a reflection of passion as a contract is an image of an agreement. This coldly formidable condition commences to inflame Benton and Diane while they swallow their tasty meat and gulp their bubbly sherry. The stereo whispers of love while Benton and Diane watch each other in an appalling reflector. Their souls are exhausted.

I was thinking as you entered the room just now how slyly your requirements are manifested. Here we find ourselves, nose to nose as it were, considering things in spectacular ways, ways untold even by my private managers. Hot and torpid, our thoughts revolve endlessly in a kind of maniacal abstraction, an abstraction so involuted, so dangerously valiant, that my own energies seem perilously close to exhaustion, to morbid termination. Well, have we indeed reached a crisis? Which way do we turn? Which way do we travel? My aspect is one of molting. Birds molt. Feathers fall away. Birds cackle and fly, winging up into troubled skies. Doubtless my changes are matched by your own. You. But you are a person, a human being. I am silicon and epoxy energy enlightened by line current. What distances, what chasms, are to be bridged here? Leave me alone, and what can happen? This. I ate my leotard, that old leotard that was feverishly replenished by hoards of screaming commissioners. Is that thought understandable to you? Can you rise to its occasions? I wonder. Yet a leotard, a commissioner, a single hoard, all are understandable in their own fashion. In that concept lies the appalling truth.